Days of Grace and Silence

A Chronicle of COVID's Long Haul

Days of Grace and Silence

A Chronicle of COVID's Long Haul

by

Ann E. Wallace

© 2024 Ann E. Wallace. All rights reserved.
This material may not be reproduced in any form, published,
reprinted, recorded, performed, broadcast,
rewritten or redistributed without
the explicit permission of Ann E. Wallace.
All such actions are strictly prohibited by law.

Cover design by Shay Culligan
Cover art by Scott Redden, "Yellow Bluff," 2007,
oil on linen, 30" x 30"
Author photo by Jennifer Brown

ISBN: 978-1-63980-514-3

Kelsay Books
502 South 1040 East, A-119
American Fork, Utah 84003
Kelsaybooks.com

For my trusted healthcare providers
and for my friends and family
who have helped me through,
again and again and again.

Acknowledgments

My gratitude to the following publications, in which versions of these poems originally appeared.

Autumn Sky Poetry Daily: "To My Students in the Time of the Novel Coronavirus," "Not Yet, Abby," "This Virus, a Villanelle," "Lilac Season," "A Wager"
Chautauqua: "Lessons I Learned This Summer"
Clementine Unbound: "An Abundance," "Sounds Will Carry"
Coffin Bell Journal: "For the House Finches," "Blessed Be," "Days of Pressure and Fog," "The Taste of Fear"
Eunoia Review: "Jigsaw," "Two Fears," "Things Begin to Break" (as "Breaking Point")
Feral: "Spring Rain"
Green Mountains Review: "Home Learning," "Passages," "The Infinity of Hope"
Halfway Down the Stairs: "The Safety Within," "Enamel" (as "Touched")
Literary Nest: "April Mud"
Michigan State University Libraries Short Edition: "The Alchemy of Survival," "Training Ground"
MockingHeart Review: "Possibility" (as "Relentless"), "One Year into the Long Tail of This Virus I Find Things I Do Not Recognize" (as "The Wearing")
New Note Poetry: "Airborne"
New Verse News: "Breathless," "Fool's Gold," "This Dangerous Place"
One Art: A Journal of Poetry: "Note to Self: Two Kindnesses, or One," "Practice," The Empty Casing," "Water World"
Panoplyzine: "Synesthesia"
Pendemics Journal: "Angle of Recovery," "Tulips"
Red Eft Review: "Rooting"
Silver Birch Press: "My Facebook Feed Tells Me"

Snapdragon: A Journal of Art and Healing: "The Silence of a Place"
Thimble Magazine: "To Live Deliberately"
Wild Roof Journal: "Flashpoint," "The Anatomy of a Storm"
Wordgathering: "Hunger," "In-Between Days," "Name I Don't Remember," "Every Night Interminable" (as "Sleepless") "Spring Song," "Ties That Bind"

With Gratitude

For my medical team who went far beyond professional duty in caring for—and *about*—me through my acute COVID infection and prolonged illness. The impact of personalized, compassionate care too often goes unnoticed and underappreciated. Suzanne Hess, APN, Jeanine Bulan, MD, Yasmin Meah, MD, Sharon McSorley, BSN, Noah Greenspan, DPT, Marion Mackles, PT, Wai Chin, MS, and the staff at Pulmonary Wellness made themselves available—whether by phone, text, online, or in person—through my most frightening and arduous moments, and for that I am deeply grateful.

For the friends and family who checked in on me (in the limited ways a pandemic allows), left food outside my door, and cheered me on from afar. I felt the love every day.

For the Long COVID community that began to take shape online in spring and summer 2020 and gathered force as our illnesses went on and on—supporting each other, sharing information, conducting research, lobbying elected leaders, and making our voices heard. As the rallying cry goes, nothing about us, without us.

For my writing community: the Colgate crew, for our Sunday morning Zoom marathons—Jennifer R. Edwards, Christina Kelly, Michael Foran, Thomas Frank and David Harris; Rebecca Barrett-Fox and the Any Good Thing writing community, which helped me develop the daily writing practice that made this collection possible; and the support, faith, and inspiration of January Gill O'Neil, David Rigsbee, Jeannie E. Roberts, Gayle Brandeis, Jules Gibbs, N. West Moss, and the many other creatives who helped shepherd this project.

For Kim Correro, my friend and WildStory partner, whose support of my writing has never wavered and whose vision is boundless.

For Jason Burch, who helped with the small things, at a time when nothing was small, and in moments of emergency alike.

For Katerina and in memory of Raya, from whom we were isolated through what we thought was the worst of it. Through loss and grief, Katia has grown strong and stronger.

For Molly and Abigail—Molly, who managed our home when illness broiled inside, and who, as spring gave way to summer, fall and beyond, was my companion in our daily walks up and down Ogden Avenue. And Abigail, whose affection and creativity brighten the dark days. No teen wants to spend so many weeks and months home with their mother, but our time together has, in so many ways, been a gift.

For Konstantin Vail, who has been by my side throughout my illness, even in the months when we needed to stay apart for safety. His pandemic experiences as a funeral director and as a son, glimpses of which can be seen in these poems, are heart wrenching. Though his sacrifices and losses have been immense, his love and compassion remain steadfast and true.

And for my parents, Janet and Vern Wallace, whom I have given more than enough medical scares for one lifetime and whose love, faith, and support for me are truly breathtaking.

Contents

The Porches of Strangers   15

Days of Pressure and Fog

Quarantined Hours	19
For the House Finches	20
Airborne	21
The War Effort	23
Breathless	24
In Danger	25
Math Problem	26
April Mud	27
To Live Deliberately	28
Possibility	29
The Safety Within	30
Blessed Be	32
To My Students in the Time of the Novel Coronavirus	33
Days of Pressure and Fog	34
If I Had a Choice	35
The Taste of Fear	36
Jigsaw	37
Every Night Interminable	38
Spring Song	39
Chest X-Ray with COVID	40

This Dangerous Place

Special Delivery	43
Fool's Gold	44
This Quarantine Kitchen Is Closed	45
Tethered	46
Another Possibility, Spring 2020	47

Isolation, Apart — 48
Not Yet, Abby — 49
Night Breathing — 51
Live, a Little — 52
Untethered — 53
Viral Rooting — 54
Rest — 55
Fathoming — 56
This Virus, a Villanelle — 57
Fourteen Weeks — 58
Home Learning — 59
This Dangerous Place — 60
An Abundance — 62
Two Fears — 63
Body Politic — 64
Life and Liberty — 65
Hunger — 66
House of Gold — 67

Sounds Will Carry

Recovery at New Year's — 71
Enamel — 72
Things Begin to Break — 73
Flashpoint — 74
Synesthesia — 75
One Year into the Long Tail of This Virus
    I Find Things I Do Not Recognize — 76
Angle of Recovery — 77
Tulips — 78
Burning — 79
Buoyed — 80
Lying Side by Side, Each Night We Part Ways — 81

Lilac Season	82
Sounds Will Carry	83
August Sun	84
Names I Don't Remember	85
Rooting	86
New Driver	87
My Facebook Feed Tells Me	88

The Infinity of Hope

Standing in a Different Place	91
The Anatomy of a Storm	92
Training Ground	93
On Being	95
The Silence of a Place	96
The Alchemy of Survival	97
What Luck	98
Imprints	99
At the Crossing	100
Lessons I Learned This Summer	101
A Wager	103
Ties That Bind	105
Note to Self: Two Kindnesses, or One	106
The Empty Casing	107
Passages	109
In-Between Days	110
Water World	111
Spring Rain	113
Practice	114
The Infinity of Hope	115

The Porches of Strangers

Thanksgiving Day, 2022—Jersey City, NJ

Life in this city does not come easy.
Some days unity seems a hard-pressed ideal formed
and held only in our isolation, together but apart,
always apart. It takes but a flash for a person enraged
by fear to wield words, or weapons, of hate, to take aim
at the fissures running through this place of multitudes.

The interior of my city block probably looks a lot
like yours—a grid of fences, the older ones chain
linked, rusted, low enough to wave and say hello over,
the newer walls tall, opaque, dividing land and light.
We've learned to mark our space, imagine silence.

Each of us has suffered, suffers still, has grieved,
in our own way, behind closed doors or before eyes
that do not see. We are of a city, of this nation,
where living is not easy. Our needs these years
have been hard and our losses harder.

Yet I have friends and you do too, who in this loud
and crowded place, toss sunflower seeds onto the dirt
at the sidewalk's edge and into empty lots, who plant
milkweed today so tomorrow's butterflies might live.

We leave meals in unlocked fridges dotted through town
the way other places have Little Libraries, with books
for the taking, and we have those too. We offer
couches, pots, pans, online to strangers.

We welcome anxious teens and land-lost refugees
into our fold and we give them love. We feed the birds
and each other, on faith we will live through to see
the beauty next year holds, together.

And when my next year, in its beauty and its losses,
was not a certainty, my friends, who are yours too,
were watching, and they came with food and more,
elixirs left in bags and foil without comment,
outside my door.

Love is found on the worn city stoops and faded porches
of strangers pulling abundance from deep within to leave
in shopping bags and survival kits marked with your name,
or mine, to be picked up without contact and without debt,
each of us an unknown neighbor bound, one to the other,
to the other.

Life in this city does not come easy. Yet it gives
from behind closed doors and in silence, neighbor
to neighbor, unnamed friends who may not say hello
when they pass on the sidewalk, but who watch
from the other side of the fence. They see the cardinal
who lives in the pear tree planted twenty years ago
when I put down roots, claimed a bit of city air,
and invited the birds to take a branch, so that we—
you and I—might listen together to their song.

Days of Pressure and Fog

Quarantined Hours

March 21, 2020

Hours bump, one into the other,
in these close and viral quarters.

Rough and stinging dawn, into midday,
into evening, into dark.

Into still, the rhythm
of my daughter's cough, unrelenting,
pushing us into night's lightless chokehold.

Into these drumbeat hours as I lie and listen,
and my lungs fill heavy,
the press
of pain
hard upon
my heart.

For the House Finches

April 1, 2020

I wonder if the house finches know
they own the yard this year—
the cheery red-headed finches,
the cardinals, sparrows, mourning doves
and the large lone pigeon who began visiting
last week as I fell ill, to peck beneath the feeder.

All of them.

They can have the yard this year I think
as I heave myself off the couch,
slip my feet into my empty red boots
pull a shawl around my shoulders
and stumble outside to offer them
some food.

Airborne

April 2, 2020

Each   breath
    breath
 beating   breath
sucks
  in
the thin
  air

Exhaustion
        floods
  the pulse

       pulse

    slow   pulse

      of the

          ex

              hale

A wave of light

    of   blue

       then   dark

  sways
      inside
          my head

           floating   right

floating   left

                     around

  around

                                                      around

The War Effort

April 3, 2020

Women across America unearth machines
from the far reaches of their homes, from dusty closets,
from moth-balled attics. They oil the gears, wind
the bobbins with cotton-covered poly, set the spools, adjust
the tension, lean in and squint to thread their needles.

They rummage through stashes of fabric, remnants
of long-ago projects, eyeball faded quilts, pull
worn t-shirts from the rag bag, smooth each piece
flat and pick their armor, as they smile grimly
and recall tales of grandmothers' victory gardens.

They find their shears, crackle measuring tapes,
download patterns, place tissue on salvaged cloth,
curl their world-weary bodies over their work
protectively, and set to flash and snip their metal
blades through tight-knit cotton swatches.

And as they baste and stitch mask after mask,
as spring turns to summer, America's women brace,
with stiff backs and strained eyes, awaiting the call
to build test labs or more in their kitchens, prepared
to fill a nations' needs as our leaders flounder and fail.

Breathless

April 4, 2020

I have spent these slow motion
weeks watching the world scramble
and panic through the screen of my phone,
held cupped in the palm of my hand.

I hold these 8 square inches in the palm
of my hand, attached to my body
confined to the length of my couch,
or my queen-sized bed up a flight of stairs

I can no longer walk without gasping
for the air flowing through the two floors
of my 1,800 square foot home,
in my city filled with 270,000 other souls,

all gasping for air, and all I need
is enough to pump through my 5'2"
body, not too much, but I can see
on my screen that I am not alone

in my need, and I can see, though
it all makes no sense, why my small body
panting and blacking out on my red couch
inside my red house cannot get enough air.

In Danger

April 5, 2020

I went to work every day prepared to die in a tiger cage.
Dying doesn't scare me. At all.
　　　　　　　　—Joe Exotic, *Tiger King*

We are all locked
inside, watching tigers
on our screens, tigers
kept in cages by men
who may be unhinged,
who go above the law
for tourists who gape in awe
at such danger so close.

We all, at home, leave
our wide mouths agape
or back up our six paces,
but we are feeling unhinged
so we plot the tigers'
escape and their freedom
instead of our own
as we sit in our cages.

We fail in our plans.
The tigers, they are still
barred in their cages,
yet it is only now,
with all of us stuck
home in our places,
that the tigers are finally
safe where they are.

Math Problem

April 7, 2020

At the start of April, a body would be held
a cold two weeks to be cremated in New York City.
Which means a family would wait those 14 burning
days for an end to the start of a nightmare.

That was a lifetime ago, last week,
when only 300 New Yorkers, give or take,
died each day, officially, of the pandemic.
And those bodies still wait in trucks
that hold 40 apiece, called into service
when hospital morgues, meant for a dozen
or so, filled just two weeks ago.

The numbers go up and up, yesterday to 731
known COVID deaths, plus the daily 200
who now die at home of undetermined causes,
with ailments like fever, like cough,
like not being able to breathe.

We are near 1000 lost each day.
But we do not like such ballpark math.

But the morgues are full,
and the refrigerated trucks,
and the cemeteries,
and funeral directors drive
vans that never sit idle or cool
as they remove body after body
after body.

Nobody wants to think about how
this all ends. But we really should
just do the math.

April Mud

April 9, 2020

I sat in my yard today for the first time
in weeks, no, the first time this spring,
and as I sat, a light rain spattered around me.

I sat a little longer, feeling the sky darken,
the shadows grow sharp, and the birds sing
more brightly, as spatters turned to drops.

While I sat, men on Hart Island in airtight
hazmat suits worked side by side in the rain,
digging muddy trenches for fresh pine boxes.

The men on Hart Island buried last month's
dead who waited two weeks, alone, unclaimed,
together in city morgues filled past capacity
to be interred in plain boxes on a wet April day
while the birds in my backyard sang.

To Live Deliberately

April 10, 2020

When I walked 'round Walden Pond
on a warm March day, I traced the foot-
print of the small cabin and wondered
about Thoreau and his solitude,
deliberate yet close to all he held dear.

Days later, home in my city,
my eldest simmered and coughed.
I gathered her and her sister, pulled
the door shut behind us and spun
a soft space where we might keep safe.

We did not know then that the thick
walls would hush and dim the sounds
of the street beyond, quiet and quieter,
and create an echo chamber for the cough
unending of my fevered daughter.

The cough resounded in each chime
of my phone, the CNN, NPR, New York
Times alerts, texts from friends, calls
from the doctor. We heard the world
shutter as she, then I, grew sick and sicker.

Alone in our city, I think of Thoreau,
of his small pond and his long saunters,
of his dear Emerson who would come
sit for a spell in the cabin in the woods,
and leave his friend replenished.

When Thoreau emerged from the woods
two years later, he was a changed man
returned to a static world. But as we fight
for sleep, for air, for life, we have no idea what
strange and silent world awaits our return.

Possibility

April 11, 202

I plumb the depths
of all we do not know,
the unspeakable terror.
Every night I am pulled
along a path that ends
in viral mass destruction.

Each dream begins
in possibility—
of a cure, of safety—
until hope is dashed, dashed,
and dashed again.

My heart pounds
me awake. I listen
to remember
where I am.

And every night
my daughter's cough—
dry, relentless—
reminds me
that we are
not yet destroyed.

The Safety Within

April 12, 2020

We dwell in this quiet
house, sealed tight from a world
grown unfamiliar over long breathless
weeks. Dry hot battles have waged
within these walls, each day won,
or lost, with the steady flood
of oxygen, to the rise and fall
of body temps and the tight
burn within my chest.

These battles
are small and
also life
and death,
but four weeks in,
the terror
has grown
familiar.

Beyond the walls
of my chest, of the beating
hearts in this house, grows untamed
terror, destruction, that we do not
yet know, that has laid bare,
will still lay waste,
to my neighbors,
my friends, my city,
and so far beyond,

and as we recover
strength
and stamina
here inside
and plot our return,
I have begun to fear
the vast weeping silence
we will find outside.

Blessed Be

April 13, 2020

The woman watched as her husband took his last
breath.

They were together, but it is small comfort
to die at home during a pandemic.

There was no peace for the man
who left his wife sick, frightened, alone
with no money
for a funeral, no money
for someone to come
and take his body.

There was no solace for the wife
when the police came, noted
her loss and left
her illness, her grief,
her love lying still in their bed.

There was too little left
for a family that had nothing but love
holding it together.

There is no comfort in dying
at home during a pandemic.

To My Students in the Time of the Novel Coronavirus

April 14, 2020

I know you are struggling, that you had
already fought and kicked to make it
to spring break, to the week when we would
all come up for air before the final push
of a hard semester. But break this year
was a last gasp, right before our class was sliced
in two—into before, into after,
when the fragile balance of everything
you were holding together, while holding
your breath, shattered, as if a cat had walked
across the shelf where your most precious
pieces were perched and casually swatted them,
one by one, to the floor. We are stuck here
frozen, staring at the glassy shards,
knowing we cannot scoop the thousand
pieces into our hands and mold them back
into January or February, when life was sharp
and fragile but not broken.

I know you are struggling, and, though I will
not tell you this, I know you will continue
to struggle. So much has shattered.

I will not tell you because you are
surrounded by shimmering dust
that reflects off your face in ways
that we could not see before. And for every
piece of you that has broken, a new angle
becomes visible. And what I know
is that you are present and fighting,
and that though you are struggling,
you will not be broken.

Days of Pressure and Fog

April 15, 2020

My daughter laughs
at my muddled questions asked
on repeat. I forget not just
the answer but that I have already
inquired about schoolwork, dinner,
the weather, what else? I cannot remember
if I have been talking to her
or to myself.

I fight to break this neural haze,
thick, so thick,
in the pulsing darkness,
noisy and closing in, always in,
on the center of clarity growing small
and smaller,
week upon week.
I close my eyes in exhaustion
against the drumming inside my head.

My brain swoons and constricts,
and I feel myself diminish
as my blood runs low
on oxygen. I fight not just for air,
but for words, for logic,
for narrative.

I fight to remember the story
of me.

If I Had a Choice

April 16, 2020

I would have picked
the flash and danger
of the fire eater who swallows
the flaming torch
and snuffs it out to riotous
applause as it plunges
from mouth to throat to lungs
over the deadly burning
inhale of this novel coronavirus.

The Taste of Fear

April 17, 2020

Look into my heavy eyes,
or imagine you can,
and see the near defeat
that has kept me here
pinned to my couch
for this 33rd day.

Listen as I read
the last words
of a friend whose stilled
and silent body
rests four days later
in the makeshift
morgue full and overflowing
outside the hospital
with the ER
that I do not want to visit,
as if *visit*
is the right word
when one is trying
not to die.

Each time I rush
to the ER, I inhale
through the paper barrier,
feel the poison
air fill my lungs,
and breathe hard
because breath
is not something
anyone would dare
to hold right now,
even for luck.

Jigsaw

April 18, 2020

I pieced together my home
state today, in a map of New England
broken into a thousand pieces before me.

I found my unmarked town
on Buzzards Bay, located Hyannis,
Falmouth, New Bedford—long ago rivals
in high school track, popped Woods Hole
and the islands into place,
laid out the Whaling Museum's mighty blue
recalled from so many school trips,
crooked the arm of the Cape
and made a fist of Provincetown.

From my quarantined living room
in New Jersey, I could have traveled
anywhere as I put together a world
by my back window, yet I chose
to go home.

Every Night Interminable

April 19, 2020

Sleep's false victory
is crushed upon waking.
I check my sleepy math
and count the short hours—
three and a half, maybe just three.
Sometimes fewer.

My hands tingle and numb,
head tightens and pounds,
fingers of pain curl
around my temples,
the pillows too hot, too thick,
twisted covers ensnare
my shoulders,
my feet boil and kick free
as I flail for comfort.

Darkness and oxygen run low
in tandem by night,
as the pressure grows fierce—
pounding, churning.
I squeeze my eyes,
cradle my skull, and stifle the wail
bubbling within.

The nights, they are interminable.
But the mornings, they are worse.

Spring Song

April 20, 2020

The sirens
wail the soundtrack
of this silent spring,
a keening intertwined with birdsong
by day,
with my daughter's dry, dry cough
through the night,
life and death bound together contrapuntal
on and on,
so that I no longer hear the sirens,
until I do.

Chest X-Ray with COVID

April 21, 2020

Stand here, back a little a stumble, a side step	he guided me into place
arms up, above your head	he raised my hands
back straight, chin up a crumple, a reach for help	he lifted my drooping head offered his hand
take a breath, let it out a heavy breath, a woozy swoon	he withdrew behind the wall for safety
again, and hold another breath, a viral wave a whoosh, a rocking side to side	he pressed the button
and let it out spine caves, body heaves for the chair, a winded collapse	he hurried back to my side took my arm and eased me down

This Dangerous Place

Special Delivery

April 22, 2020

An oxygen tank arrives
by special delivery.

Now I recover?

Fool's Gold

April 23, 2020

The president wondered aloud
if we might wipe out the pandemic
with disinfectant, like we swipe
over doorknobs and countertops,
sprayed inside our bodies, or
with tremendous amounts of light.

This, on the day my oxygen
tank was brought to my doorstep
by a man who could not enter
my infected home, could not step
past the tub of chlorine bleach wipes
that I leave outside my door.

Tomorrow, may I wake rested,
my blood fortified and ready to wipe
clean the virus running loose within me,
and may I not read of devout red, white,
and blue Americans drawn to the
bright light of this fatal fool's gold.

This Quarantine Kitchen Is Closed

April 24, 2020

I stocked up at the start
with produce for soup and pasta,
for hearty salads, bought three kinds
of potatoes.

I never dreamed everything
would rot where it lay
before I began to recover.

Tethered

April 25, 2020

Fifty feet of green tubing
ties me to home base, the tank
plugged into the outskirts
of my kitchen, from which I roam
my short distances inside
the narrow confines
of my quarantined home.

Fifty feet of tubing
provides far more length
than I can ably cover
on my short leash
of this month's stamina.

Another Possibility, Spring 2020

April 26, 2020

If only we could hibernate
our way through the long spring
into summer to wake come fall
slimmed down, the virus shed
and gone, to breathe deep and free,
wondering if it were but a nightmare,
and stagger from our familial
dens into the bleary dawn of golden
autumn, forage the neighborhood
for bits of food, and learn the art
of bare bones living and gratitude
that might carry us through
the winter of our reemergence.

Isolation, Apart

April 28, 2020

This unyielding wall of isolation
divides us for safety,
me from you,
you from me.

My viral load in quarantine.
Your essential risk in circulation.

Two separate terrors
experienced alone, alone.

Not Yet, Abby

April 29, 2020

When my youngest was just three, or maybe four,
I took her to the dentist one morning in early November.

Before we left the house, she plucked a bright red lollipop
from her Halloween bag and held it out, posing a silent question.

You can't eat that now, Abby,
I said as I lifted her into her car seat.

She held it tight in her small fist as we drove,
left it safe in her cup holder when we went in for the cleaning.

Back in the car, she held up the candy,
Now, Mommy?

Not yet, Abby,
I replied as we drove to her preschool.

I left her chattering with her friends and went to work.
Half past five, I rushed back to the little school.

As I walked through the heavy front doors,
I saw she had been waiting.

She ran to me and held out her tightly curled fist,
palm up.

She unrolled her fingers to reveal her red lollipop,
still in its wrapper.

Now?
I laughed. *Yes, but first, let's put your coat on.*

A decade later, six weeks into a pandemic,
Abby quietly opens her bedroom window and slips outside

to sit in the afternoon sun, perched in safety on her fire escape.
At thirteen, she already knows the answer to the question

she has not bothered to ask—
Not yet, Abby.

Night Breathing

April 30, 2020

In viral night, the crash of waves,
a rush and pull, floods my head
when daytime sounds of close quarter
living have quelled and silenced for a spell.

The whoosh of air pumps through
each inhale,   pulsing,   exhale,   pulsing
the roll and crash,
                roll and crash,

that lulls me fore,
                    and swings me back,

awash,   so light,
        circling,
                circling   into dawn.

Live, a Little

May 3, 2020

I see it unfold through my window—
the gray rains of April yield to a pool
of sunshine, finally here. We have grown
antsy as cold and foul weather held us in,
as the virus washed over and took
root in some homes but not others.
But the healthy are now ready to flaunt
their pent-up luck, to dance in the god rays.

To live a little. It is all anyone wants,
all the awakening dancers can think now
that spring is here. But it is an old refrain
for the COVID-sick, who have breathed
our wish so humble—to live, just a little
longer, and then, a little more.

Untethered

May 6, 2020

When I gave birth to my oldest,
her father hesitated to cut
the cord, afraid his hand might
shake, cause harm with a slice
made in error. We laughed—
what could go wrong?

For eight weeks, I have strung
new tethers, kept my girls close
inside where we three feel safe,
even as infection brews hot
within these walls. I fight
to fill my lungs, and their father
brings food and leaves us
to recover within our silo.

As health buds into spring,
we open the doors, and I urge
one, then the other, to venture
forth, hesitant, masked, and back
again. We no longer laugh
at all that could go wrong.

Viral Rooting

May 11, 2020

The news keeps
breaking, the symptoms
unfurling
down my palm-
sized screen, this insomnia-
inducing bedtime

reading list.
It blurs my vision.
Head spinning,
heart beating
fast, I feel the pressure build,
check my oxygen.

It's an old
habit now eight weeks
in, yet still
fresh terror
as this viral knowledge takes
root inside of me.

Rest

May 21, 2020

My shut-in lungs
are weary,

so weary from each
stale breath,

tired too
of oxygen,

concentrated
and rhythmic,

pushing into me
when my whole

body just wants
to slow

for a heavy
beat.

Fathoming

June 5, 2020

I cannot make sense
of people gathering
plans to reopen
as if 100,000, plus
20,000 more, plus
the uncountable
uncounted
have not died,
as if the lives saved
are not because we
kept our distance
and stayed home.

I cannot fathom
those laying out
plans like bodies
in their caskets,
as if we who did
not die are not still
healing our scarred
and pummeled bodies,
and learning to breathe
once more.

This Virus, a Villanelle

June 8, 2020

I've come to think of this virus as a mad villanelle,
like Sisyphus staggering up the hill under his stone
each week tumbling backward into hell.

For months I've heard the siren's new death knell,
contrapuntal to my breath's stuttered tone—
and therein lie the rhythms of this virus, a villanelle.

An unending circling round, each wretched swell
pushes me down, as I gasp for air alone
tumbling backward into these waves of hell.

At dawn, I renew my feeble fight to expel
the infection rooted within its pulsing home,
every gain dashed by this virus, the sour villanelle.

Over months, my breath grows stronger and body able,
but the respite's a tease, relapse now so known,
Yet, each slip a surprise, a tumble back into hell.

And more, when I finally bid this disease its long farewell,
leave my sickbed to see what the world has sown
I fear I'll see how fast we have fallen back into hell,
that it's we, not the virus, who've created this tortured villanelle.

Fourteen Weeks

June 15, 2020

I didn't lose track of just the numbered days—
and after 80 or 90, who wouldn't?—
No, like a new mother tracking time by weeks
until counting by sevens grows dizzying,

who turns to months as her babe sprouts teeth,
rolls over, and claims a spot in the world,
I have lost my place in this circling of sleepless
nights, of nameless days, of too little air.

Past three months, the fire in my lungs now quiets
to an ember for a spell. I try to recount the burn,
yet memory fails and the terror fades. I cannot recall
each hazy short-breathed week that brought me here.

Near the end of my viral course, I am unsure when
the vital turn happened, but I must have faith it did.

Home Learning

June 15, 2020

There is no lesson here
that my parents could have taught me.

There is no lesson here
that I can teach my children.

Except find your air
and breathe.

This Dangerous Place

July 30, 2020

We are standing
in a very dangerous place
calling the children to peer over the edge
of the precipice
as if it is a class trip
to the Grand Canyon.

We call out *be safe,*
don't go too far,
but also
don't lag.
Yet we know
that when one falls,
others,
perhaps we,
will follow,
linked arm
to arm
like a barrel
of plastic monkeys
tossed
over the edge.

And though many
will break free,
catch themselves
on ledges and clamber up
scraped,
battered, bruised,

to laugh at the close
call or scoff
that it was nothing,
a breeze even,
some
will fall
all the way down.

An Abundance

August 3, 2020

This winter spring summer
has been a long haul of suffering
and silence, of sickbed days on repeat,

with life pared down to its essence,
my attention focused on the fragile act
of breathing in, then out, for four beats,

in, out, speaking, cooking, bathing
hefty efforts to be weighed each day,
any one jettisoned for the other.

Yet amid the scarcity, a stream of love,
of care, has flowed to my small and quiet place
within this solitary house of quarantine.

Two Fears

August 8, 2020

for Konstantin

Could you ever understand if you were not
here in this quiet place of fear with me?
Behind these doors locked tight to keep you safe
and separate, the walls proved too porous
to hold life elements of oxygen, of sleep.

Each day rose and fell with the rhythms
of tossing tumbling night, pulsing mud-gray
dawn, head in hands begging the pain
to ease, the daylight struggle for air, voice,
strength, gasping for reason, for tomorrow.

Could I ever understand that these doors
locked tight did not just divide the fear,
mine from yours, but multiplied it?
That the view from the other side of the pane
left you, too, gasping for reason, for hope, for air.

Body Politic

August 27, 2020

This body
aches, has ached, is
still hurting,
the compounding
months of hot, viral assault
flashing on, off, on.

Perhaps soon,
this body might run,
but breathing
deep and hard,
will need to rest, to inhale,
and refresh airways

vacated
and left to stiffen
as we lay
dormant or
dying, one or the other,
while our nation tried

to heal, 'til
suffering soured
into scorn,
and the slow
down ended before we learned
how to breathe anew.

Life and Liberty

October 3, 2020

The sirens are running
at night again.

I wonder for whom
they cry.

Hunger

November 25, 2020

I suck in each brittle breath,
as my windpipe closes
around the thin flow
that sticks at the base of my throat,
then sears into my waiting lungs.

We call it air hunger.

Is this what suffocation
feels like, or maybe
drowning?

House of Gold

November 26, 2020

after Twenty-One Pilots

My daughter texted me, "I have a video
of her. She's singing House of Gold."
And when the file loaded, I took a breath,
pressed play, picked up another apple
to peel for our Thanksgiving pie and watched

as my daughter's friend sang, a tall girl seated
upright in a folding chair, singing, like you might
see at a school assembly anywhere, but different.
I counted back in time, three years, to the moment
Ellie sat in that chair and sang of growing old,

and the tears crept down my face unstopped
by my hands peeling, peeling green apples
for our pared down Thanksgiving meal
in a fragile year of disease and mourning.
You would think we'd be used to it all by now.

As I wiped my face and returned to my work,
I gave small thanks that we still come undone
by the gut punch reminder of a beautiful girl,
who once invited us to turn our future upside
down and think we might live ever after happily.

Sounds Will Carry

Recovery at New Year's

January 1, 2021

Despair and fatigue sit deeper
than bone, yoked together
in a battle of wills against
hope and faith, whom I keep
nudging to step up, chest out,
hands on hips, and deliver
a knockout punch to last year,
that year of tremendous loss
and suffering, which was just
yesterday, and all it is paying
forward into the new one.

The year of hope and faith
in science, in change, in breath,
has lost round one in this house,
as I was sucked in the undertow
of yesterday, vomiting
and sleeping off stomach-
turning pain killers
that I won't soon be ready
to abandon as my slow recovery
unfolds in its own sweet time.

Enamel

Winter, 2021

I held her hand cupped within mine,
her brown fingers curled in permanent rest
as I applied a fresh coat of enamel to her nails.

I did not know the frail woman in the casket,
though I wrapped her body in the fine sari
her family brought, pulled silver bangles

onto her wrists and brushed her hair. And I held
her cool hands in mine as I painted her nails,
wondering when her skin had last been touched,

in life and without worry. And I thought of the long
viral months when my skin too was untouchable,
and I pressed the warmth of my palm into hers.

Things Begin to Break

Spring, 2021

one year into this long haul,
the weight of each new day's neglect

adding upon that of the one before
and before and before,

since the time before this virus
entered my home uninvited.

But what do my appliances or wifi router
or bathroom sink have on my spirit?

Let them break.
I will outlast them all.

Flashpoint

Spring, 2021

Some years, spring's greatest
deceptions are daffodils
and cherry trees flashing
their gaudy colors
before a blizzard,
sparking benign outrage
among the lucky
who don't know to hush
and hold hope
that we might pass
through these weeks
of growth and tumult
unscathed.

Synesthesia

Spring, 2021

I was thinking about hungry birds
and spring and the returned fever
of my daughter but these things
do not inspire hope

so her sister suggests music
and plays a song she says
is orange and pink
and sounds like a painting

and now I know
we both hear color
and texture
when others are stuck
listening for the words.

One Year into the Long Tail of This Virus I Find Things I Do Not Recognize

Spring, 2021

Veins bulging that once lay flat, flaccid pouches
where muscle lived and flexed, fine lines
and crepe-draped skin puckering
above the vee of my shirt. I have plucked
stray white hairs from my temples,
dabbed flesh-toned cream on the dark
hollows beneath my eyes, been awakened
each night by hot pain gripping
my arms, shoulders, head.

I am learning to find solace
in the wearing of my flesh,
in the pulsing reminders of this hard
fought year, each one a mark
proclaiming that I am still here.

Angle of Recovery

Spring, 2021

for Marion Mackles

She learned in the early 90s
that the sidewalks of New York
are not flat, taking her handheld
level to the pavement to find
how hard it was for the weakened
still beautiful men to walk the avenues
they had owned just years before
and plot a course for their return.

And now, as I walk uphill indoors,
focused on breath and stamina
and the sloped city blocks
I might soon traverse
outside the sunlit seventh floor
window, I think of the angles
she measured to make living just
a little bit easier for those long gone
men filled with a hope like mine.

Tulips

April 8, 2021

This month is known for the unflinching
bind of life and death. My Aprils
have crescendoed into despair
each more deafening than the last.

It was just yesterday that I fed
the birds and tossed the wilted tulips
that had brightened my home for a week
and almost bought a dozen more.

I had no idea what fresh despair
today would bring.

Next week, I will glass-eye a squirrel
who tips the scales of backyard feeder
and hangs tight as he gorges on sunflower
seeds meant for cardinals and sparrows.

Your mother's ashes will be delivered
from the crematory and left in a box
at the funeral home, to be scattered
come fall in the piney woods at the Cape.

I will think of you and the weight
of that slight box as I sit by the window
and watch a handful of addled birds
peck for food at the emptied feeder.

Burning

Spring, 2021

The box is cardboard
but strong enough to hold
your mother and the hands
that once held you in her lap
in a faraway city
a long time ago, smiling
forever in black and white.

The box is cardboard
but stuffed full with roses
and calla lilies, the scent
escaping as we slide it
from the back of the van
and hand it off
to the attendant.
I want to tell him
of the sweetness within.

The box is cardboard
and burns as we drive
away, heat searing
through you as grief does
even after we reach
the highway, even as
we arrive home,
and it will continue to burn
long after the ashes
have cooled to white.

Buoyed

Spring, 2021

A decade ago I sailed
upon still waters
that lasted half a beat
before gale forces
toppled and pushed
me down
and down
again.

But in the drowning
I buoyed
alone, adrift
and made my way
to a new shore.

Lying Side by Side, Each Night We Part Ways

Spring, 2021

You, into vivid nightmares, a cruel loop
of imagined mother-son arguments
that never end, never resolve, of your hand
reaching to touch your mother's,
your waking hours' distress
brought to bear in grief-filled slumber.

Me, alert and pinned in place
by viral agony, unable to toss
or to turn, and rarely falling
into sleep, the bedsheets too heavy
to pull atop me, body pained
and pulsing, hour upon hour.

We surface together every few hours,
pass a forlorn and weary look,
and try again to prove that the nights
might not always be such torture.

Lilac Season

Spring, 2021

for Raya

As spring arrived once more,
the death calls petered out.
We made it through a full year,
just barely, and survived.

Scarred and struggling, we let down
our guard, celebrated our escape.

The final blow came then
in the thirteenth month, shots
burning fresh in our arms, cherry
trees gaudy in their pink finery.

Our joy as foolish, death ordinary
and unexpected would not stop.

Come lilac season, we swiped
a sprig or two from untended
side gardens and held the purple
blooms to our unmasked noses.

We inhaled the sweetness, so strong
and fleeting, and wept for you.

Sounds Will Carry

Summer, 2021

We have pulled at thin air and breathed
in the shallows, hungry, our hearts
and lungs ablaze, commanded ourselves
to breathe, and breathe some more.

Our breath sounds swallowed
by the wail of sirens, on and on, the fear
stuck in our throats has now crescendoed
into the guttural cries of a nation in grief.

But we have laughed
as we have cried.
And we will laugh,
and we will cry some more.

And the sounds will carry us,
like calling cards of the lost and bereft,
across the bridges and through the cities
in search of each other.

August Sun

Summer, 2021

I have lost too many springs,
too many April, May, June
days in hospital beds, recovering
or barely surviving at home,
as new life swirled into action.

I have watched the cherry tree
in my yard burst into pink,
the finches and robins return
to peck for seeds in the blooming
spit of green outside my window.

I have returned to pluck sparrows'
bloated bodies from my pond,
to shovel limp mourning doves
downed by the looming hawk
into heavy contractor bags.

As spring rains pool and flood
my backyard patio I remember late
summer years ago. My water broke right
there, my body tightening under the August
sun with the pain of new life coming.

Names I Don't Remember

Summer, 2021

I dressed her in a white sari
and painted her nails,
but I do not remember
her name.

And I don't
remember the name
of the man whose cheeks
were stained purple
with pooled blood
from lying prone,
a ventilator
strapped to his face,
as he lay dying
and dying and dying.

I do not remember their names,
but I remember her
delicate nails and graying hair
that I combed smooth
behind her resting head,
and I remember his face,
marked by signs of a fate
that might have been mine.

Rooting

Summer, 2021

Your birthday was full
and happy, your skin
aglow from a day
of sun and water.

And yet you carried
a muddled frustration,
a rooting, an unnamed
yearning.

By day's end,
nothing satisfied.
You wanted
more.

It has been four months
and you are still
learning new ways
to miss your mother.

New Driver

Summer, 2021

Walking, like breathing,
is not yet easy.

Last year the tick tock of teenage
progress came to an unwelcome stop,
and the world closed up
as my daughter, then I, fought for air.

But as spring gave way
to the steady warmth of June,
we reemerged together
to make our way, halting,
up and down our mile-
long street, counting
our breath, in and out,
checking oxygen,
and speaking
of times ahead,
waiting on our return.

Our long illnesses
relapse and persist,
and I am trying,
with my small energy, each day
walking up and down our street.

My daughter though,
she drives now, away,
away, from Ogden Avenue
and reminders of our long virus.

And in the car, it is easy
to forget that walking
still holds the power
to take her breath away.

My Facebook Feed Tells Me

Summer, 2021

that milkweed and butterflies
are this year's sourdough bread
and backyard chickens
as the pandemic has turned
our attention from life
that must be kneaded and tended
each day and in earnest,
filling solitary days, one
after the other,
with small tasks
and gratification that is in sight
but does not come quick
or easy. A year in, we take
a breath and make
space for the wild things
that pollinate and multiply
when we step aside
and let them be,
reclaiming once
manicured city slips
of greenery
as the early pandemic
bakers and hen handlers
now relax into gathering seed pods
for next year's bees and planting
parsley for the swallowtail
caterpillars to munch,
each doing its job without ado
as we learn to withdraw
our heavy hand.

The Infinity of Hope

Standing in a Different Place

Spring, 2022

I have not strayed far
from home, the tether
of my oxygen held taut
for too long, now flagging,
since a warm March
lap around Walden Pond before
it all shut down and my home
became a pulsing hotbed
of virus, of illness for weeks
turned to months to years.

I have not strayed far
and yet the world has
tilted on its axis, and I have too.
I scan the once-flat ground
for a new toehold
where I might find modest
purchase, take a breath and release
my tether, then engage these weary
muscles and reach
my hand up high
from my precious ledge,
groping for a new patch
of solid ground.

The Anatomy of a Storm

Spring, 2022

The way Minnesotans know snow,
deep, intimate, without fear,
is a lesson on living through
the squalls of these middle years.

Some decades are winter through
and through. But after a spell
we build a home within the storm,
nestle under the crystalline shards,
light a match against the too-early
dark, and stop waiting for the sun.

Training Ground

Spring, 2022

Each decade, or sooner,
I've been granted a fresh chance
to master the art of illness.

I cut the teeth of adulthood
with a tumor and an ovary
dissected in the lab, a bare head,
and a fridge full of chemo.
My doctor called me kid,
and she was not wrong.

The fragile pact of my survivor
story dissolved in my thirties,
my body dizzy, trembling,
a new disease scratching
at frayed nerves within
my head. Chaos called for focus
upon the art of living, even
as my world spun
fast and faster.

When a third disease took
root, the humility of losing
another organ gave way
to the painful art of healing.

But I was ready for the latest
blow, had braced myself
when the heat and weight
of the virus descended,
shuttered my home
first among my neighbors,

bringing fear that each labored
breath might be my last.
As this long tail storms, a trail
of wreckage left within me,
I pick up my pen
and stop waiting
for my long recovery.

On Being

Spring, 2022

I find old to do lists saved
in my phone, from fall 2016,
summer 2019, and more, seasons
that overwhelmed, easy items
ticked off, the harder goals abandoned.
The story of each why
is long forgotten—or not,
the satisfaction of completion
suspended, the weight
never lifted.

In these two years since
we all pulled to a stop, those lists
have become remnants
of a past that no longer serves.
I fill my phone now with notes, bits
of research so my body might heal,
but also lines like poetry
from people mastering
the art of healing.

In these suffering months
I have learned to stop making
lists of all I must do. I am learning
to simply be.

The Silence of a Place

Spring, 2022

We have all learned to hear
silence these years, but the quiet
that beats within is ours alone,
mine from yours, yours from mine.

The silence of each place
is different. You might locate
yourself by listening for how
the earth pulses beneath your feet.

The Alchemy of Survival

Spring, 2022

The science was there,
in the chemo cocktail that dripped
into me for five days each month,
a regimen my body bucked
and fought until the drugs
were no longer needed.

I grew strong, learned to see the world
anew in the light refracted
off the shards of my weary soul.

And I fell sick again. And again.
Each time, I tinkered, trying to spark
an ember from basest of metals, dark
and lifeless, until the smallest flare
of hope caught fire and I bent over,
cupped my hands around the flame
and blew gently until it danced.

What Luck

Spring, 2022

We know to count our blessings
and nothing more, to say thank you
for not losing everything along with
our health, as if because we are sick
we should be grateful for life itself.

And I am.

But what a country where luck
amid illness is measured by hardships
dodged, a mortgage not defaulted,
meals not missed, where we have all
but given up on finding a cure.

Imprints

Spring, 2022

The fragile imprint of my twenty-two-year-old
body sears into my breathless middle-aged flesh.

Oxygen tubing mimics the tether of the IV
pole I dragged through my first apartment,

as saline dripped into me, flushed toxic
chemicals that saved my life decades ago.

These years I live in the shadow of my past.
The confines of home, large, comfortable, shrink

to the 600-square-foot one-bedroom that held me
through six months of chemo, as I fought

for energy to walk down four flights
to my city stoop and step into the sunlight.

At the Crossing

Spring, 2022

The language
of this place, like the wind
is not gentle,
and it is loud
as it whips around us.
We stand here in the middle

of a bridge
above fast waters.
The road slopes
toward land
to the right, to the left,
but the language of this place,

like the wind,
is not gentle, and
we are tired.
We stand here
in the middle of a bridge,
and it is not a gentle place.

Lessons I Learned This Summer

Summer, 2022

One.

If you hold a detested spotted lanternfly
in your closed fist, then throw it
on the ground, it will become disoriented
long enough for you to stomp on it.
But first you must not be afraid to catch it.

Wipe your shoes and do not despair—
you are helping save the trees.

Two.

Overwhelm has been transformed
from a verb into a noun by self-care gurus
peddling master classes and high fives online.
It names the swampy place that holds you fast,
there in front of your screen
until you find the power to log off,
go outside, and listen for your own soft voice
too long silenced by the din.

Three.

To reclaim the sanctity of a space,
you must be ruthless, rip out
the invasive, and replant with seeds
and tender shoots that have always sat
quiet and overlooked on this bit of earth.
You need not do this all in one day.

Four.

The boldest step is the first step,
small but intentional, of your feet
pointed off the crowded path
into the untrampled understory.

Trust the next steps to come
more easily.

A Wager

Autumn, 2022

An empty trail is easy to follow.
I seek the company of shedding
trees, their branches laid bare
as these pared down years stretch
into my fifties. I forage along the moss
and leaf-loamed forest floor, find fall
berries and mushrooms, excited even
by inedible finds filled with toxins
or bugs, take my photos
and move on down the trail,
ever in search of the mottled
light that touches each still dangling leaf
and trunk, that makes the plain browns,
the dull reds of autumn shimmer and glow.

An empty trail is easy to follow,
easier to trust than those
who may not believe that we—
and by we in this extended moment
I mean me, but also you—
are worth protecting. The social
contract derided, ditched,
if it ever existed at all, so I get lost
for a spell in the brush and bramble,
to breathe deep, easy, even
as I pant and fight to fill
my spike-scarred lungs on the long uphill.

Shadows stretch and the sun
sinks low. I follow the path
as it bends toward home.
My survival skills are finely honed,
but not for this life of roots and snares.

No, I, like you, have sharpened
my senses, have placed
my wager on one more day.
I must leave these woods and learn
to walk alone amid the smiling faces.
But I remember—
an empty trail is easy to follow.

Ties That Bind

Spring, 2023

This illness breaks me
into three tied and tattered
threads—mine, hers, theirs,

a long narrative that ruptures,
compounds once, then
again, just when

we thought it all was
coming to its overdue
post-viral close.

One mother, two
daughters, three
years apart in birth

and now in illness.
Nothing alike, but in this
wretched timeline

sixteen is an age
of possibility spoiled
and spoiled again.

This ending remains
out of reach and it
does not resolve

with an easy breath
or a wish blown
upon a candle.

Note to Self: Two Kindnesses, or One

Spring, 2023

Do you get as frustrated as I
that some lessons do not come easy
or fast, that there are things we know
deep in our bodies, that we have learned
through trial and error and error
and error, and yet
we must learn them again?

I think you know,
this feeling of carving
out space, of creating
sanctuary within your home,
your body, of finding
the necessary beauty of silence,
but then inviting the noise to rush in
when a friend calls for help.

I struggle here, to find
the line between kindnesses—
between being a good human
and being good to myself. And truly,
why do those things feel at odds,
and how might I lift my gaze
upon myself if I held a line
here, between you and me?

But what I really want to say
is that I think our needs
are mutual and that maybe
this note to self is a reminder
to ask for help in claiming
silence.

The Empty Casing

Spring, 2023

Imagine this: if you have planters
of parsley or dill growing outside
in a sunny spot, odds are good
that you have tossed butterfly eggs
onto your pasta with the garnish
or mixed them into your salad.

Just imagine.

Have you ever seen the egg
of a butterfly? Before caterpillar,
before chrysalis. The miniscule sphere,
a perfect glassy orb deposited
by swallowtail or monarch or fritillary,
and perched so delicately on a leaf
or the whisper-thin stem
of your garden herbs.

I saw my first last summer.
I watched as the brilliant swallowtail—
she visited daily for a spell—found
my bed of parsley. I searched
for a week, leaf by leaf until
I spotted it: one perfect egg.

How small, how fragile.
How large my hands,
my garden shears—the egg stood
such small chance against a quick
snip at mealtime. Small chance
against hot sun that can wither
a wispy herb into the parched earth
over a few dry days of drought.

It is truly a wonder
we have any butterflies at all.
But my patio egg, it defied the odds—
it hatched under my protective gaze,
grew fat off the parsley I did not eat,
spun a home around itself.

I watched and waited as it grew strong
Then one morning I found
the empty dry casing still stuck
to the side of my clay planter.
The butterfly—it was gone, flown
away into its new life.

Passages

Spring, 2023

It's been decades since
my body held a narrative
clear and simple. It turned
to poetry long ago, when
a refrain emerged, was
repeated with life
interrupted once, then
again, and again.

A poem always begins
in the middle, or someplace
nearby, because truly, have you
ever tried telling a poet
to begin at the beginning?

When doctors ask me,
or my daughters, how
our illnesses began, oh,
the poems we compose
on paper-lined examination
tables, each one of us a stanza
braided to the other to the other,
with no beginning and no end.

The poet in me dares not ask,
if we are always muddling
around in the endless looping
middle of this story, how
might we ever write our way out?

In-Between Days

Spring, 2023

Each day here
coughs
and sputters, runs low
on fuel, just like before

but worse

because
the experts proclaim
this chapter has come
to a close.

Water World

Spring, 2023

The dreamy images flashed
in quick succession, on and on,
recognizable but too fast
for reading the endless
pages of fine print.

Awake, but not, I thought
I'd caught myself dreaming,
was sure that this medical flipbook
must be rapid eye movement.
Drifting back to sleep, I told myself,
I must remember this.

My next thought, upon waking—
do other people see medical bills,
one after the other, after the other,
inscribed within their eyes
while they sleep,
or at least try to?
Do they dream of static images,
of text and debts?

While the numbers
and the fine print spread
before me,
my daughter, still sick
in her bed, dreamed
in fear and senses,
of waking to the pressure
of water trapped within her walls,
of the sheetrock growing soft
and moist to the touch,

of hazy thoughts that she could rest
just a few minutes longer, that she had
more time to act, more time
before the liquid pocket burst
like a balloon all over her bed,
soaking her, as she recounted later,
in dirty wall water.

But she was wrong, time was short,
and the walls in her dream gave way
before she could get out of bed.
And the documents in mine kept scrolling.

Spring Rain

Spring, 2023

Last fall's dried leaves quietly snapped
and crackled on the forest floor,
yes, like cereal in milk.
I knelt, placed my ear
to the earth, and listened.

A rain too light to feel
was falling, faintly popping
against the brown and brittle leaves.
I held out my open palm. Nothing.
But the ground continued to speak

and a moist loamy scent lifted
in the air. I inhaled, raised myself up,
and soon the drops came fat
and fast enough to touch.

Practice

Spring, 2023

I think I had the whole thing
wrong.

Again, again, again.
I thought it was about me,

that I was the end point
of these battles

through chemo and vertigo,
that three decades of knowledge

were meant to save
me.

Turns out, my dry run
held a different purpose:

when first one daughter,
and then a second,

fell sick and sicker,
I should have been ready.

The Infinity of Hope

Spring, 2023

We talk a lot about the little things,
the ripple of a stone in the glossy surface
of a lake, circles pushing out and out
and out, until they join other
circles and waves, each a disruption
that begins with the weight of an object
thrown or body, say of a dragonfly,
landed where before there was none.

We talk a lot about the little things,
the small decisions or delays that mean
you and not me, or me and not you,
is in the wrong, or the right, place
at the wrong, or the right, time.

We used to call it chaos theory,
the way one small action here
has grand potential to impact you,
wherever, whoever, you may be.

Sometimes the ripples, they are
devastating, the wave of one airborne
particle, heading toward me and mine,
the way we might think an action
is harmless because we do not think
to look where that stone lands, where
the ripple travels, because we are
so mesmerized by the rings expanding
with perfection upon the smooth water.

But other times the impact
of the small things, it is beautiful,
a kindness or surprise that spreads

like a ripple into a smile, a day set
into motion, expansive, unknowable,
with potential that is infinite.

So tell me, what small ripples
will you release into the world
today on faith that you may not see
what stuck things they loosen?

About the Author

Ann E. Wallace, PhD is the 2023–24 Poet Laureate of Jersey City, New Jersey. As a long-time survivor of ovarian cancer, a woman with multiple sclerosis, and one of the nation's first Long COVID patients, she has lived and written through illness for thirty years. Pain, disability, and disease—as well as hope and resilience—have inspired and informed her work as a poet, memoirist, patient advocate, and scholar. *Days of Grace and Silence* was written over three years, beginning when Wallace was first sick with severe acute COVID and following her teenage daughters' and her long journey of recovery. Wallace's first collection of poetry, *Counting by Sevens* (Main Street Rag, 2019), is a reflection on motherhood, illness, and contemporary life in America.

Wallace is host and producer of *The WildStory: A Podcast of Poetry and Plants* by the Native Plant Society of New Jersey and Professor of English at New Jersey City University. She grew up in a large family in the small waterfront town of Marion, Massachusetts, migrated to New Jersey to study art at Drew University, and never left. She holds a master's degree in Women's Studies from Rutgers University and a doctorate in English from the Graduate Center of The City University of New York.

Her work is online at:
AnnWallacePhD.com

and on Instagram:
@AnnWallace409

For information on Long COVID,
visit the NIH RECOVER Initiative at:
RecoverCOVID.org

www.ingramcontent.com/pod-product-compliance
Lightning Source LLC
Chambersburg PA
CBHW022145160426

43197CB00009B/1433